Wild Mountain Tribe

A 14-Week Quest to Capture Masculinity. Together.

WILD MOUNTAIN TRIBE
is a guidebook for men to use in conjunction with
THE WILD MAN fable.

© 2016 by Zeke Pipher
Printed in the United States of America

All rights reserved. No part of this publication may be reproduced, stored in a retrieval system, or transmitted in any form or by any means—for example, electronic, photocopy, or recording—without the prior written permission of the author and/or publisher. The only exception is brief quotations in printed reviews.

Scripture quotations are from the ESV® Bible (The Holy Bible, English Standard Version®), copyright © 2001 by Crossway, a publishing ministry of Good News Publishers. Used by permission. All rights reserved.

Order *Wild Mountain Tribe* or *The Wild Man* fable
at www.thewildmountain.com or www.zekepipher.com.

WILD MOUNTAIN PRESS
www.thewildmountain.com

ISBN 978-0-9979627-0-1

Table of Contents

Foreword by Bryan Clark.. 4
What is Wild Mountain Tribe 5
A Word About Masculinity 6
Preparation for the Journey 8
Role of the Facilitator 11
Note to Pastors and Men's Ministry Leaders............................... 13
Tribal Discussions: 14-week Overview 15
Tribal Discussions
    Week 1..17
    Week 2... 21
    Week 3... 25
    Week 4... 29
    Week 5... 33
    Week 6... 37
    Week 7..41
    Week 8... 45
    Week 9... 49
    Week 10.. 53
    Week 11.. 57
    Week 12.. 61
    Week 13.. 65
    Week 14.. 69
Wild Mountain Feast 73
Acknowledgments... 75

FOREWORD

There have been unique challenges in each generation. One particular point of confusion in our current culture is what it means to be masculine. There is a difference between simply being male and being a man. One is predetermined genetically and one is cultivated over time. I believe Zeke has properly identified a significant area of confusion in today's culture. What does it mean to be a man? What does it mean to be a "Wild Man?" How do we separate out the confusion of the culture and return to God's intent in making a child uniquely male, on purpose for a purpose? This journey requires more than simply content taught in a classroom. It is more of an adventure that older men take together with younger men to discover that part of themselves that is fearfully and wonderfully made by God. This journey is not for the timid or faint of heart. It's an adventure for men of all ages, young and old, who want to be all that God created them to be.

Take the journey if you dare. You won't be disappointed.

Bryan Clark
Pastor, Lincoln Berean Church
www.lincolnberean.org

WHAT IS WILD MOUNTAIN TRIBE?

You are holding a guidebook. *Wild Mountain Tribe* helps men—young and old—explore the terrain of masculinity together. *Wild Mountain Tribe* also provides older men an opportunity to initiate younger men into the sacred fraternity of manhood. In his book, *Iron John*, Robert Bly describes the process of initiation into manhood employed by the Kikuyu tribe in Kenya. When a boy is ready to become a man, the adult men in the tribe take him away from the village—away from his mother, sisters, and all the other comforts of his boyhood world—and they lead him to a sacred place where only the men go. They require the boy to fast for three days, and then on the third night, they join him around a campfire—a tribe of elders and one hungry boy.

The initiation begins when one of the older men takes out a knife and opens a vein in his own arm. He collects some of his blood in a gourd and passes the knife and gourd to the next man. That man takes the knife and does the same thing. The cutting and the collecting continues until each adult male in the tribe has contributed to the bowl. At that point, the bowl is passed to the boy, and he is invited to satisfy his hunger by drinking from the gourd.

That may sound gruesome to our "civilized" minds, but the young man learns several valuable lessons through this ceremony. He discovers that his elders take seriously their responsibility to pass on masculinity; so seriously, in fact, that they're willing to bleed for it. He learns that only men can initiate boys into manhood. He sees that a knife can be used for deep and wholesome purposes, and not merely for playing or fighting. He also gains a picture of how blood represents the life of another person and how, through the blood of his elders, he has been invited into the life of every man in his tribe.

Wild Mountain Tribe gives older men a chance to bleed for younger men, taking their responsibility to pass along masculinity seriously. *Wild Mountain Tribe* gives men of all ages a chance to open their hearts, minds, and histories, and pour themselves into the lives of other men.

A Word on Masculinity

In *The Wild Man* fable, masculinity is represented by hair and physical strength. However, you do not need to have a beard or large biceps to be masculine. Many of the young men who read *The Wild Man* and *Wild Mountain Tribe* are years away from being able to grow facial hair or bench press impressive weights. Likewise, many of the older men who read these books have lost the thick hair and physical abilities of their youth. Neither situation limits a man's opportunity to be wild. Many authors and speakers have reduced the definition of masculinity down to haircuts, clothing styles, and physical abilities. This narrow, external-focused explanation of masculinity pushes many of our manliest men out of the category, and that is a sad, unnecessary loss.

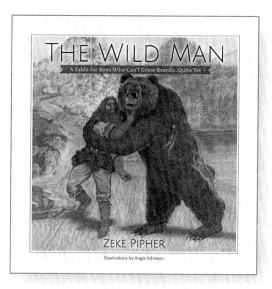

To be masculine is to carry the right vision, do the right things, and follow the right King. Being masculine does involve being strong, but strength takes many forms. The fraternity of wild men is varied, abundant, and multi-sided — You will find that it has plenty of room for your style, abilities, and skill-set as a man.

PREPARATION FOR THE JOURNEY

1 FORM a tribe of friends and family.

A "tribe" is a large family or a group of companions that share the same customs, convictions, and values. The first step in this *Wild Mountain Tribe* adventure involves inviting a small group of men to be a part of your tribe. Your tribe will consist of a few older men (fathers, grandfathers, and father-figures) and a few younger men (sons, grandsons, and young men in need of father-figures). Some tribes will consist of a few fathers and a few sons, but not all tribes will look this way. Young men need wisdom and vision from older men, and sometimes the older men are active, engaged fathers. But, this isn't always possible. When a father-son teaching relationship isn't possible, it falls to grandfathers, uncles, or other father-figures to hand on a vision for masculinity. *Wild Mountain Tribe* is a journey for all men who want to cast a vision for what it looks like to live a truly masculine—truly *wild*—life as a man of God.

As you gather a tribe, it's important to keep in mind the main two objectives for this journey:

1) This journey is designed to help men hold important discussions about masculinity. This book will raise far more questions than it will answer. *Wild Mountain Tribe* isn't aiming to resolve all issues concerning masculinity; but it will help men have important discussions *with* people they love and respect.

2) The second objective for *Wild Mountain Tribe* is to help men—young

and old—develop strong, supportive friendships. We all desire to have brother-to-brother relationships, but only men striving toward the same vision find it. CS Lewis writes: *"The very condition of having Friends is that we should want something else besides friends... Those who have nothing can share nothing; those who are going nowhere can have no fellow-travellers."*[1] *Wild Mountain Tribe* gives men a chance to go somewhere together.

2 READ *The Wild Man* fable by Zeke Pipher.

Our journey begins with a fable. Nothing holds the power to direct our lives like the tales we tell ourselves. Fables remind us of what we want, and what is possible. G.K. Chesterton writes about bogey, the imaginary evil character that carries off naughty children: "Fairy tales do not give the child his first idea of bogey. What fairy tales give the child is his first clear idea of the possibility of defeat of bogey."[2]

The *Wild Man* fable illuminates some of our culture's most threatening bogeymen, and shows men—young and old—that together, with the Lord's help, they can be killed. Many of the images and phrases used in the *Wild Mountain Tribe* have been taken directly from *The Wild Man*, so it is important to have everyone read The Wild Man fable before taking the *Wild Mountain Tribe* journey.

3 SELECT a sacred space for your tribe to meet.

Rooms, structures, and spaces communicate vision to us, telling us what to expect while we are inside. For example, when you enter a comfortable living room, you sense it's a place to relax and let your guard down. Conversely, when you enter a cold, marble-floored structure, you know that it's designed to host formal events. A football stadium tells us we're likely going to cheer. A library informs us that we're going to need to be quiet.

These tribal discussions are unique, so you may want to choose to hold them someplace unique, such as a corner of an old barn, a sportsmen's club, or around a fire pit in a back yard.

4 MEET with your tribe once a week for 14-weeks.

Plan to meet together as a tribe each week for about two hours. Each tribal discussion involves reading a few thoughts at the beginning of the section, and then having a discussion together as a tribe based on the questions provided. There will be a time for prayer at the end of each tribal discussion.

5 PERSONALIZE your adventure.

This is your journey with your tribe, so find ways to personalize this adventure and make it exciting. Consider having the older men go fourteen weeks without shaving. Perhaps encourage everyone to wear the same shirt or hat to each weekly discussion. You may want to add additional Scripture memory challenges, service projects, or masculinity challenges to your journey. Have fun, be creative, and make the most of these fourteen weeks together.

6 FEAST together.

At the end of the 14-weeks, the older men will have an opportunity to plan a *Wild Mountain Feast* to celebrate the conclusion of this quest, and initiate the young men into the ancient fraternity of wild masculinity.

1) CS Lewis, *The Four Loves* (New York: Harcourt Brace & Company, 1988), 66-67.
2) G.K. Chesterton, *Tremendous Trifles*, Book XVII: The Red Angel, 1909.

Role of the Tribal Facilitator

Direct the process of forming a tribe.

Someone needs to invite men into a tribe, and this is often the role of the facilitator. A tribe might consist of two dads and two sons, or it could contain any combination of grandfathers, fathers, sons, father-figures, and young men who need father-figures. In order to have good interactions each week, the ideal size for a tribe is between 4-10 participants total.

Host a Tribal Council of Ancients.

Before a tribe begins their 14-week journey, the facilitator might consider calling the older men in each tribe to meet once in order to set a vision for the trip and pray for the upcoming discussions. Many older men will feel challenged, or even intimidated, by this journey toward masculinity. That's perfectly normal, and the facilitator can use this pre-trip meeting to help each man know that he's in good company. (See the next section for thoughts on what to share during the first meeting.)

Create a safe environment.

The facilitator doesn't need to lead every meeting, but will be responsible for inviting men—young and old—into the tribe, and for setting the tone of the group. Paul Tillich said, "The first duty of love is to listen." The facilitator is primarily responsible for helping each man—young and old—find a chance to speak, and a chance to listen. The facilitator should regularly remind the group that the discussions that happen within a tribe are confidential. Trust is vital for a tribe to develop strong relationships and move closer to the Wild Mountain.

Point men back to Jesus.

The facilitator doesn't need to solve his tribe members' problems, or have vast insights into the topics that will be discussed. The facilitator is merely responsible for making sure that every person in the tribe feels welcomed and valued, and that everyone gets a chance to speak and respond to others. God, through the help of the Holy Spirit, in the context of strong relationships, will encourage, inspire, and renew men during this journey to the Wild Mountain. The weight of healing men's hearts and inspiring them to be wild is not on the facilitator's shoulders. It's on the Lord's, and He is always faithful.

Note for Pastors and Men's Ministry Leaders

Wild Mountain Tribe was designed in part to be used by churches, college ministries, parachurch organizations, and various other men's groups. If you are considering forming tribes from your community, it might be a good idea to hold a pre-meeting (Tribal Council of Ancients) for the fathers/father-figures in the group. Many of the discussions that men will have together on this journey will be challenging. Some men will be asked to verbalize thoughts and feelings they have never spoken aloud before or will be encouraged to engage their sons and grandsons in new ways. For these reasons, it might be helpful for a pastor or leader to address the older men before the 14-week journey begins in order to communicate a few important ideas, such as:

- You are free to share with your tribe as much as you'd like, but you are not under any pressure to divulge information. These tribal discussions must not pressure or manipulate anyone into saying something they might regret later. Part of building trust with one another involves allowing each man to freely choose what he is comfortable sharing with his tribe.

- No one person should dominate a tribe's discussions. The goal for these tribal discussions is to hear from everyone, and so it's important that each participant focuses as much attention to listening as they do to talking.

- These discussions will surface issues and memories that are sometimes painful. We all have regrets, and we all have sin in our lives that we wish we could get rid of. It's important for men to know that they're not alone in feeling regret or conviction of sin, and that there is grace and forgiveness for absolutely every issue that might surface on the journey toward the Wild Mountain.

- The pastor or leader may need to broaden the vision for who is welcome in this 14-week journey. This trip to masculinity is not merely for fathers and sons; it is also designed to help grandfathers connect with grandsons, or for father-figures to help encourage other young men who need a mentor in their lives. Many men—young and old—are longing for a father-figure or mentor, but they haven't found that need met by their biological fathers. This journey is designed so that any mature older man could step into that father-figure role.

Tribal Discussions
14-Week Overview

WEEK 1: Wild versus savage. This discussion explores the difference between being masculine and being macho.

WEEK 2: Father-hunger. This discussion explores the universal longing for a father, and how those desires, met or unmet, help us develop a strong relationship with God as our Father.

WEEK 3: What makes a man measure up? This discussion explores the difference between living by grace versus living a self-focused, performance-oriented life.

WEEK 4: Owning Up. This discussion explores how the path to freedom and relationship begins with being honest about our sins.

WEEK 5: Fleeing the Seductive Stranger. This discussion explores how we can say no to sexual temptation through the power of God's grace.

WEEK 6: A wild man's view of women. This discussion explores how a truly masculine man views women.

WEEK 7: Fleeing the Foolishly Fun Stranger. This discussion explores our temptation to avoid work and responsibility, and how the path of life requires we be responsible and do our work.

WEEK 8: Warriorhood. This discussion explores how, to be *wild*, we must stand against evil and fight for the weak and vulnerable in our world.

WEEK 9: The great will kneel. This discussion explores how Jesus destroyed and replaced the world's definition of greatness.

WEEK 10: Willing to be lonely. This discussion explores how faithful leaders will walk alone at times.

WEEK 11: "I've got your back!" This discussion explores how grace enables men to have life-giving friendships.

WEEK 12: Choosing heroes carefully. This discussion explores how we are likely to become like the heroes we choose.

WEEK 13: Wild and disciplined. This discussion explores the paradox that to be truly wild and free, we must submit to the authority of Father in Heaven.

WEEK 14: Torchbearers. This discussion explores the responsibility older men have to pass along a vision for masculinity to younger men.

- WEEK 1 -

WILD VERSUS SAVAGE

READ OUT LOUD AS A GROUP:

"The true power that is available to us, the power that multiplies power, lies on the other side of the choice to empty ourselves of power."
— Andy Crouch, *Playing God*

"He has told you, O man, what is good; and what does the LORD require of you but to do justice, and to love kindness, and to walk humbly with your God?"
— Micah 6:8

Savage men are brutish, rude, and cruel. They are prideful about their masculinity and use their strength—voices, bodies, or positions—to dominate others. For this reason, a savage man's power is something others fear, and for good reason; savage men are known to abuse and hurt other people in their aggressive pursuit of ego.

In contrast, wild men are powerful, and even at times fierce, but they are always kind and self-controlled. The wild man's power has been transformed by the love of God. He no longer lives for himself; he now exists to care for others with the unselfish and sacrificial concern that God first showed him. Wild men are something to behold today, a rare sight. They are wise, fair, realistic, compassionate, and assertive on behalf of all things good and true. At the center of their hearts, wild men carry a white-hot ember that burns for the glory of God. This ember is hotter than the flames of hell, and it fuels wild men's passion to serve and protect others.

Our culture presents several confusing, and often conflicting, definitions of masculinity. Through video games, violent movies, ego-filled sports stars, and power-hungry politicians, young men experience thousands of images and examples of savage men each week. This is not healthy. This does not help young men form a vision for becoming a strong, ego-less, responsible men. As older men, we must present a different vision to our sons, grandsons, and other young men in our community—living examples of how rich, varied, and flourishing masculinity can be. That is precisely what we will do over the next fourteen weeks. We will grow wilder. Together.

DISCUSS TOGETHER

1) In *The Wild Man* fable, how did the Wild Man and the Ancient Man display power? Did their power benefit others, or harm others?

2) Can you think of one time recently that you used your power to serve or protect others?

3) Can you think of one time recently that you used your power in a selfish way, perhaps to intimidate someone?

4) When you think about our culture—celebrities, political leaders, athletes,

and artists—how do you think our society defines masculinity?

5) What do you agree with, or disagree with, about our culture's definition of masculinity?

6) Can you think of a man in your life who seems to be faithfully living out Micah 6:8 by doing justice, loving kindness, and walking humbly with his God? Describe him.

PRAY TOGETHER

Have one of the older men in your tribe read 1 Timothy 4:8. Close in prayer, asking God to give each man a vision for being a faithful, masculine, truly wild man.

WILD MOUNTAIN TRIBE CHALLENGE

Do one thing each day this week to serve someone else. For example, consider doing a sibling's chores for him/her, washing the dishes for your wife, or mowing your neighbor's lawn. Choose one simple, practical way to use your strength to be kind to someone each day this week.

WEEK 2

FATHER-HUNGER

READ OUT LOUD AS A GROUP:

When the father-table, the groundwater, drops, so to speak, and there is too little father, instead of too much father, the sons find themselves in a new situation. What do they do: drill for new father water, ration the father water, hoard it, distill mother water into father water? — Robert Bly, *Iron John*

"I cannot think of any need in childhood as strong as the need for a father's protection." — Sigmund Freud

"Brothers, join in imitating me, and keep your eyes on those who walk according to the example you have in us." — Philippians 3:17

All of us are born with a hunger for a father. Just as our bodies need salt, water, and various nutrients, a boy's heart craves a father's love. This necessarily means that a father, or father-figure, is the only one who can satisfy this specific longing. This reality doesn't diminish the contribution or value of mothers, yet as hard as mothers may try they cannot impart what only fathers were designed to provide.

This father-hunger creates two realities. First, with such an intense appetite comes a great potential for hunger pangs. Indeed, many of us live with father-wounds because our longings for our dads weren't satisfied. A second reality created by this need involves our expectations; precisely because we carry such weighty hopes for our fathers, our dads are bound to fail us. Most fathers carry a strong desire to be all their sons need, and yet they see disappointment in their sons' eyes from not quite measuring up.

These two difficult realities caused by our father-hunger lead us to two important truths as we journey to the Wild Mountain:

1. First, we need to show each other grace. As we journey toward the Wild Mountain together, we must try to understand one another. We must imagine one another's experiences of life and allow that imagination to create empathy and compassion in our hearts. Moral imagination is not always easy, or instinctive, but it is an essential part of becoming truly wild, masculine men.

As we consider each other, we will find many opportunities to ask for forgiveness, grant forgiveness, and receive forgiveness. This is also difficult. Some of us have been deeply wounded by our father's anger, abuse, and addictions. Some of us have been hurt by our sons. There is no way to sugar-coat the reality that the journey toward masculinity is hard. It requires us to tap into the deep vein of God's grace and mercy toward us so that we might show that same grace and mercy to each other. But we have to come to terms with the fact that however difficult, the path of grace is the only one that leads to the Wild Mountain.

2. Secondly, men need to let their Father in Heaven meet their deepest father-hunger. It's important to see that our father-hunger and father-wounds present tremendous opportunities to find deep satisfaction in our relationship to our Father in Heaven. All of us—as grandfathers, fathers, sons, and the fatherless—have the opportunity to cry out, "Abba! Father!" from our hearts because we have found what we crave most deeply in God as our Father.

The beauty of this is that the more we see God meet our father-hunger, the more grace and mercy we can show to our fathers on earth. When God is our Father, we can finally stop expecting the impossible from our flawed, finite fathers on earth. This frees us to be wild as sons. This frees us to be wild as fathers. And this frees us to be wild *together*.

DISCUSS TOGETHER

1) From last week's Wild Mountain Tribe Challenge: Describe a couple opportunities God gave you last week to use your power to be kind to, or sacrifice for, someone.

2) What is a quality or attribute that you admire about your own father, or the primary father-figure in your life? If possible, describe a memory of your father that helps you demonstrate that quality or attribute.

3) For the older men to answer: When you think about yourself as a father, or father-figure, what is one thing that you wish you did better, or had done differently?

4) In Romans 8:15, Paul tells us that the Spirit of God gives a person of faith a sense of sonship. Paul writes, *"...but you have received the Spirit of adoption as sons, by whom we cry, 'Abba! Father!'*

Do you find it hard or easy to think about God as your Father? Explain why.

5) In *The Wild Man* fable, Keon needed to find men beyond his family and village to show him what a father's love looks like. Describe one person, other than your father, who has helped you understand the idea of fatherly love.

PRAY TOGETHER

Have one of the older men in your tribe read Romans 8:12-17. Close in prayer, asking God to give each man in your tribe a heart that can sincerely cry out, "Abba! Father!"

WILD MOUNTAIN TRIBE CHALLENGE

The challenge for this week is to write a short letter to your father, or a father-figure, telling him a few things you admire about him.

- WEEK 3 -

WHAT MAKES A MAN MEASURE UP?

READ OUT LOUD AS A GROUP:

"Nobody's ever gone the distance with Creed, and if I can go that distance, you see, and that bell rings and I'm still standin', I'm gonna know for the first time in my life, see, that I weren't just another bum from the neighborhood."
— Rocky Balboa, Rocky

"For our sake he made him to be sin who knew no sin, so that in him we might become the righteousness of God." — 2 Corinthians 5:21

"And to the one who does not work but trusts him who justifies the ungodly, his faith is counted as righteousness..." — Romans 4:5

In the movie, *Rocky*, the main character, Rocky Balboa, was driven to prove he measured up by achieving great things. The movie was a hit because we could all relate to his pressure to perform. I was ten years old when I first watched *Rocky*. When the movie ended, I cracked two eggs into a drinking glass like Rocky had, gagged a little as I swallowed them quickly, then did ten pushups on the red shag carpet in my bedroom. As I stood in front of my mirror, flexing the non-existent muscles on my stringy arms, I thought, "I don't want to be just another bum from the neighborhood either."

This performance-oriented way of life began the moment Adam and Eve lost their relationship with God. Before sin uprooted them from their Creator, they didn't question their significance. But with sin, all humanity lost their relationship to their Source of life and acceptance. Yet, no one can live without significance and acceptance, so where do we turn when we can no longer turn to God? The only place we know: *ourselves*. We look to our accomplishments, results, and performance to try to feel worthy or acceptable.

Many of us men believe the lie that we are just a few major accomplishments from finally proving to ourselves that we measure up. So, we keep striving, focusing on our work, honing our performance, and anxiously weighing the results. This will never work, and deep inside, if we're honest, we know this is true. Enough will never be enough, no matter how great the results. Rocky illustrates this point. The Italian Stallion *did* go twelve rounds with Apollo Creed. Thousands of people cheered him on as he became Philadelphia's favorite son. The city made a statue of him. But, did these things finally prove to Rocky that he wasn't a bum?

The fact that we have another five Rocky movies suggests that they didn't. That same angst of unfinished work shows up in every movie that followed. The Italian Stallion kept knocking down enemies and breaking through barriers. He kept producing bigger and better results, yet he never found rest.

The only way for us to find rest and know once and for all that we measure up is by applying and appropriating the grace of God into every aspect of life. Faith in Jesus is trusting that the work is done. Jesus did it. The man of God could never be "just another bum from the neighborhood." Through faith, he is the "righteousness of God (2 Cor. 5:21b)."

DISCUSS TOGETHER

1) Rocky tried to find his significance and acceptance through gaining success in the boxing ring. What are the achievements and accomplishments (i.e. titles, awards, abilities, earnings, etc.) that you tend to look to in order to feel significant and acceptable?

2) Have someone read Romans 3:21-26. What makes a man righteous, significant, and acceptable according to this passage?

3) Why is it so difficult for us to believe that we measure up APART from our accomplishments?

4) When we base our sense of self on our performance, we tend to either be too hard on ourselves (insecurity), or too prideful (arrogance). Do you tend to punish yourself when you don't perform well, or celebrate yourself too much when you do? Feel free to give a recent example.

5) In *The Wild Man* fable, the Wild Man enjoys his strength, but doesn't need to prove to himself or other people that he measures up. How does this free him up to serve and protect other people?

PRAY TOGETHER

Close in prayer asking God to open your eyes to the ways that you are trying to measure up through your performance and achievements. Ask your Father in Heaven to convince your heart that you fully measure up *by grace*, and not by the works you do.

WILD MOUNTAIN TRIBE CHALLENGE

Pray each day this week for each member of your tribe that God would help them live by grace instead of performance.

– WEEK 4 –

OWNING UP

READ OUT LOUD AS A GROUP:

"Hardly anything else reveals so well the fear and uncertainty among men as the length to which they will go to hide their true selves from each other and even from their own eyes." — A.W. Tozer, *That Incredible Christian*

"There is nothing that binds us so firmly as the chains we have broken." — Howard Thurman

"Whoever conceals his transgressions will not prosper, but he who confesses and forsakes them will obtain mercy." — Proverbs 28:13

Near my house in central Nebraska, the deer have created a network of game trails along the Platte River. Whitetails typically walk the same path as they move from their beds to their feeding ground, wearing a deep rut into the soft, sandy soil. Once a game trail is established, deer rarely take a different route. They are creatures of habit.

We also are creatures of habit, and many of us have chosen hurtful paths of thought and lifestyle that we have a hard time escaping. We all mess up.

Many of us have made choices that we regret, but inexplicably, we continue to make them over and over again. We long to change, but our feet feel cemented by shame to the same futile paths.

It doesn't need to be this way. We can leave our old ways for a new trail. But there is only one way to do this—to jump the ruts and follow the path of life we must be honest about our sins. To journey to the Wild Mountain, we need to own up to who we are and what we've done. No more blaming our past. No more blaming other people. No more blaming our habits, addictions, genetics, and history. To walk with God as fearless men begins with humility and confession. It begins with owning up. Only then will we be ready to forge new trails.

DISCUSS TOGETHER

1) Have someone read 1 John 1:9. The path to forgiveness and righteousness is simple, but many men struggle to take it. Why do you think it is so difficult for men to be honest with God and others about their sins and weaknesses?

2) How does owning up to our sins help us feel close to God again?

3) How does feeling close to God help us want to walk in the paths of righteousness, saying no to sin and temptation?

4) What are a few of the common ruts that men fall into today?
How does *The Wild Man* fable illustrate a few of these cultural problems?

5) Do you believe that it is possible for you to leave your ruts once and for all by confessing your sins and walking in the grace of God? Why, or why not?

PRAY TOGETHER

Have one of the older men in your tribe read Psalm 51:1-5. Close in prayer, asking God to give each man in your tribe a humble heart that is not afraid to own up to his sins.

WILD MOUNTAIN TRIBE CHALLENGE

The challenge for this week is to ask for forgiveness from someone in your life you have wronged or hurt. As you go through the week, look for the opportunity to own up to your sin or offense by gently and humbly asking for forgiveness.

- WEEK 5 -

FLEEING THE SEDUCTIVE STRANGER

READ OUT LOUD AS A GROUP:

"God does not 'hate' sex; he hates faithless sex with forbidden women, but he loves faithful sexual expressions in the context of marriage. God loves it so much that he commands, not just that it happen, but that it be enjoyed to the point of intoxication." — Heath Lambert, *Finally Free*

"For the lips of a forbidden woman drip honey, and her speech is smoother than oil, but in the end she is bitter as wormwood, sharp as a two-edged sword." — Proverbs 5:3-4

If you feel dirty, you'll likely stay dirty. In fact, if you feel dirty, you'll likely choose to get dirtier. Why not? If you're already a mess, why not get messier? This is what using pornography and entertaining lustful thoughts does to us men. It makes us feel soiled, ashamed, and unlovable. It doesn't matter that the world tells us pornography is harmless. It doesn't matter how many times we hear the message, "Boys will be boys. It's ok." When we use porn, we feel dirty.

In *The Wild Man* fable, the Wild Man lives free in a way that many men long for, but can barely imagine. He stands on the Looking Rock, breathing crisp, mountain air deep into his lungs. He roars. He feasts. He wrestles bears for pleasure. But, he also enjoys a clear conscience. As men, the pleasure of feeling clean and whole and right with the Lord is a large part of enjoying our salvation and our masculinity.

No matter what our experiences with pornography have been, the Gospel beckons us to believe that God can change us. We can be forgiven. We can be set free. And, equally important, we can stay free. There's no reason we can't ascend the Wild Mountain, climb the Looking Rock, and roar the roar of freedom. To get there, we simply must believe that the power that raised Christ from the dead gives us victory over pornography and sexual temptation of every kind.

DISCUSS TOGETHER

1) In *The Wild Man* fable, the Seductive Stranger had a cluster of lifeless men in his, or her, shadow. How does our involvement with pornography and sexual immorality steal our joy and put us in the shadows?

2) Have someone read 2 Corinthians 7:8-11. What role does godly sorrow and repentance play in helping us feel clean?

3) What are some ways that we can help one another as men turn from pornography and lust in all forms in order to pursue faithfulness to Jesus?

4) Have someone read Philippians 4:8. Practically speaking, what does it look

like to take our lustful thoughts captive, and redirect them toward things that are pure?

5) Do you believe that it is possible, by God's grace and help, not to sin in these areas of sexual temptation?

6) Have someone read Romans 6:7, 14. What do these two verses tell us about the possibility of never sinning again in these areas?

PRAY TOGETHER

Pray together that God would convince you of the life-changing power of the Gospel, and show you how, by grace, you can live a life that is free from pornography.

WILD MOUNTAIN TRIBE CHALLENGE

Read Proverbs 5 each day this week and ask God to give you the strength and wisdom to say no to sexual temptation..

– WEEK 6 –

A WILD MAN'S VIEW OF WOMEN

READ OUT LOUD AS A GROUP:

"God assigns as a duty to every man the dignity of every woman."
— Pope John Paul II

"So God created man in his own image, in the image of God he created him; male and female he created them."
— Genesis 1:27

Throughout the centuries, in almost every civilization, women have been taken advantage of and exploited. We see this today in our society in a number of ways. As we discussed last week, the porn industry is training the minds of millions of men to view women as objects. This is a horrifying and dangerous situation, especially for the women in our lives. When men view women as objects, it places our wives, daughters, sisters, and women friends in a tremendously vulnerable situation. Objects can be discarded, ignored, intimidated, or abused.

In the book of Genesis, God created Adam and Eve to be different, but *equal* in worth and honor. He gave men and women unique but complementary strengths and roles. When God called Eve Adam's "helper," He ascribed to all wives an honorable title. In fact, the Hebrew word, translated in Genesis 2:18 as "helper," is a title that God often uses to describe *Himself.* For example, in Psalm 33:20, the Psalmist says, "Our soul waits for the LORD; he is our help and our shield." The word "help" in that Psalm is the same word God uses to describe Eve in Genesis 2:18. "Helper" is an honorable label, celebrating the indispensable importance of women.

To be wild men, we need to appreciate that the value of women is not determined by us, or by our culture. It is determined by God alone, and He has declared that women, along with men, were made in His image. What's more, through the process of creation described in Genesis 1-2, God has shown us that women are to be cherished. When God made Eve to meet Adam's desire for companionship, we see in Eve God's own desire for companionship. In the great narrative of creation, Eve represents all humanity, and how loved and cherished we are by our Creator. This is an honorable role God gave to Eve, and it is yet another way God declares the value and worth of all women.

As wild men, we must stand up and roar into the face of our culture, or into the face of savage men who threaten to degrade or devalue the women in our lives. We must declare that women deserve honor. And, whenever the opportunity arises, we must work to change what is broken and what makes women vulnerable in our society today.

DISCUSS TOGETHER

1) What are a few ways that our society makes women feel vulnerable, taken advantage of, or devalued?

2) Have someone read 1 Peter 3:7. "Weaker vessels" in this verse likely refers to how men, in general, are physically stronger than women. It might also be referring to the vulnerability that women often experience in society because of various structures and cultural norms.

   With that in mind, what does it look like for us as men to treat women as equals, while owning our responsibility to care for, serve, and protect them?

3) In our first tribal meeting, we discussed the difference between being Wild and being Savage. How do you think that wild men will treat women differently than savage men?

4) How can we help the women in our lives-our daughters, sisters, wives and/or girlfriends, mothers—flourish?

5) Describe a friend or father-figure who has shown you a truly masculine attitude toward women.

PRAY TOGETHER

Pray together that God would convict you of your sins against women, and help you view the women in your life as your Father in Heaven views them.

WILD MOUNTAIN TRIBE CHALLENGE

The challenge for the week is for each man to pick one woman—young or old— and ask her this question:

Please describe a man who, at some point in your life, made you feel valued and honored. How did he make you feel his way?

- WEEK 7 -

FLEEING THE FOOLISHLY FUN STRANGER

READ OUT LOUD AS A GROUP:

"Young men who spend their time watching violent movies and playing video games aren't very easily going to become the men they were meant to become. They will drift. They will lose out on the very reason they were brought into this world: to be great, to be heroes themselves."
– Eric Metaxas, *7 Men: And the Secret of Their Greatness*

"When I was a child, I spoke like a child, I thought like a child, I reasoned like a child. When I became a man, I gave up childish ways." – 1 Corinthians 13:11

We are seeing an epidemic of irresponsible men today. Boys—often in their 20's, 30's, and 40's—drifting from job to job, watching television or playing video games all night, trying to meet relational needs through social media and sexual needs through pornography. They're living in the bodies of adults, but thinking with the mindset of toddlers. They shirk responsibility and throw a fit when someone takes a toy away.

To live as wild men, we must trade in our childish habits for the mindset of masculinity. We must choose, in every moment, to be responsible. To do our work. To honor our commitments. To take care of what is necessary before we rest or play. This mindset of masculinity takes a tremendous discipline of the will, but leads to the pleasure of productivity. Harry Emerson Fosdick writes, "No horse gets anywhere until he is harnessed. No steam or gas ever drives anything until it is confined. No Niagara is ever turned into light and power until it is tunneled. No life ever grows great until it is focused, dedicated, disciplined."

God made us to contribute to our community. Our fundamental endeavor as people created in the image of God is to work, cultivate, and create in ways that bring honor to the One who made us. There is a time and a place for having fun, but if that's all we exist for, we're living foolish lives.

DISCUSS TOGETHER

1) In *The Wild Man* fable, the Foolishly Fun Stranger also had a group of lifeless men in his shadow. How does being irresponsible steal our joy and put us in the shadows?

2) When do you feel most tempted to set aside your responsibilities in order to play and have fun?

3) Who does it most affect, or hurt, when you play too much or too often?

4) Who in your life is a good example of a man who knows how to work and contribute, yet have fun at appropriate times? Describe this man.

5) Have someone read 1 Corinthians 13:11-12. In these two verses, Paul connects

giving up childish ways with seeing God one day face-to-face. How does the fact that we will be with the Lord soon cause us to stay focused, diligent, and responsible right now?

PRAY TOGETHER

Pray together that God would give you the wisdom to know when it's time to work and serve others, and when it's appropriate to play and relax. Ask the Lord to give you a desire to love others well by being responsible men.

WILD MOUNTAIN TRIBE CHALLENGE

The challenge for the week is to pick three chores, or home or auto repair issues, that you have been putting off... and do them.

– WEEK 8 –

WARRIORHOOD

READ OUT LOUD AS A GROUP:

"So we live in a culture where strength is feared and where there is a sense that—to protect the weak—strength must be weakened. When this happens, the heroic and true nature of strength is much forgotten. It leads to a world of men who aren't really men. Instead they are just two kinds of boys: boasting, loudmouthed bullies or soft, emasculated pseudo-men."
– Eric Metaxas, *7 Men and the Secret of Their Greatness*

"In the little world in which children have their existence... there is nothing so finely perceived and so finely felt as injustice." – Charles Dickens

"Be watchful, stand firm in the faith, act like men, be strong."
– 1 Corinthians 16:13

The Apostle Paul says in 1 Corinthians 16:13 that we are to, "act like men." What does that mean? That's one of the great questions our culture is trying to answer today. Considering Paul as a man, clearly this isn't a command to be savage or brutish. Paul would not tell us to talk tough, walk with your chest puffed out, or be controlling and demanding of others. Paul wasn't that kind of man, so he certainly isn't encouraging us to be either. No, when Paul tells us to, "act like men," he's telling us to be masculine as Jesus was masculine. Jesus is Paul's example for everything, including how to act like a man.

When we look to Jesus, we see a warrior who is both strong, and tender. He's driven by His commitment to be faithful to His Father, and by His sincere love for other people. As a warrior, Jesus humbled Himself, leaving the infinite pleasures of heaven to come to earth on a rescue mission. As a warrior, He saw our need, and at great personal cost—*His life*—He provided a way for us to be made righteous and gain eternal life. As a warrior, He didn't fear man, or what men might do to Him. As a warrior, He stood for justice, rescuing the mistreated, elevating the marginalized, and caring for those in need. And as a warrior, He tenderly and courageously addressed untruths in His culture, because ideas that are false steal life and joy.

As we discussed last week, wild men do not live as if this world is a playground for their distraction and amusement. One of the reasons God has called us to work and serve is that there are so many people in this world who need us to be warriors, as Jesus was a warrior. Orphans in Haiti, Uganda, and China need us to be warriors. Young boys and girls in the sex-slave industry in Africa, the Middle East, and Asia need us to be warriors. The Syrian refugees showing up on our shores need us to be warriors. Single mothers, children in the foster care system, the sick and the poor, they all need us to be warriors as Jesus was a warrior. Strong and full of faith, taking our orders from our Father in Heaven.

DISCUSS TOGETHER

1) Have someone read 1 Corinthians 16:13-14. In these two verses, Paul connects acting like men with doing everything in love. How does being a warrior like Jesus enable us to love the people in our lives?

2) In *The Wild Man*, the men are hiding in the shadows of the cellar. When Keon wants to do the right thing, they encourage him to "do nothing." Do you recognize this attitude in our culture today? If so, how does it show up?

3) Can you think of a time that you stood up for, or cared for, a poor, mistreated, marginalized, or vulnerable person? Describe that moment and how you felt when you were faithful.

4) Jesus said, *"And do not fear those who kill the body but cannot kill the soul. Rather fear him who can destroy both soul and body in hell. (Matt. 10:28)"* How does fearing God help us not fear man?

5) In addition to Jesus, describe one person—perhaps a character from a book or a movie—who demonstrates warriorhood?

PRAY TOGETHER

Pray together that God would give you the heart of a warrior.

WILD MOUNTAIN TRIBE CHALLENGE

The challenge for the week is for your tribe to make a financial contribution to an organization that is caring for widows, orphans, foster children, or refugees (I.e., Compassion International – www.compassion.com, International Justice Mission – www.ijm.org, Samaritan's Purse – www.samaritanspurse.org, or Show Hope – www.showhope.org).

    Along with making a donation, have each member of your tribe pray for that organization each day this week.

– WEEK 9 –

THE GREAT WILL KNEEL

READ OUT LOUD AS A GROUP:

"Do you wish to rise? Begin by descending. You plan a tower that will pierce the clouds? Lay first the foundation of humility." – Augustine

"Not everyone can be famous but everyone can be great because greatness is determined by service. You only need a heart full of grace and a soul generated by love." – Martin Luther King Jr.

"But whoever would be great among you must be your servant, and whoever would be first among you must be slave of all." – Mark 10:43b-44

In *The Wild Man* fable, Keon doesn't go looking for greatness; he seeks only to protect his village. However, because he put others first, he was given the awesome responsibility of becoming the next Wild Man. This is the path to becoming *great* in the kingdom of God—when our goal is to seek to serve, not be served, we display the values and qualities of our Savior.

The world tells us that we demonstrate our worth by getting into the end zones of life, demanding that the camera be pointed at us, and performing flashy victory dances. According to the world, we prove our success and importance through scoring baskets, acing tests, earning large incomes, and owning expensive possessions.

God's definition of greatness is completely different from the world's. Jesus said, "Whoever wants to be great among you must be your servant." When He said this, He wasn't merely tweaking the world's power structures; He was dismantling them. "Servant" isn't a glamorous title. Servants wash feet, scrub toilets, change diapers, do the dishes, help with homework, mow the lawn, clean up cat puke, and rub tired necks at the end of long days. Servants work in the shadows, when the cameras *aren't* rolling. Servants live to please their master. And servants aim, not at their own greatness, but at loving others, even at great personal cost to themselves. This is how Jesus was great. And this is the path to greatness all wild men must take, as well.

DISCUSS TOGETHER

1) Have someone read Luke 22:27. What are some of the ways that Jesus served His friends and family?

2) What role did suffering play in Jesus' service to us?

3) What are ways we might suffer if we make ourselves servants of the people in our lives? Are you willing to suffer in these ways?

4) Do you struggle with the idea of being a servant? What is it about these ideas that poses a challenge?

5) Describe a man or woman in your life who follows Jesus' example of true greatness.

PRAY TOGETHER

Have someone in your tribe read Galatians 5:13. Pray together that God would redefine greatness in your mind and heart, and give you opportunities to serve other people this week.

WILD MOUNTAIN TRIBE CHALLENGE

The challenge for this week involves two tasks:

- Give some amount of money to someone in need *anonymously*.
- Pick one of the dirtiest, grossest, or most undesirable chores in your home or workplace, and do it with gladness, knowing that you are following the example of Jesus, the greatest Wild Man to ever walk this earth.

WEEK 10

WILLING TO STAND ALONE

READ OUT LOUD AS A GROUP:

"Life always gets harder toward the summit – the cold increases, responsibility increases." – Friedrich Nietzsche, *Twilight of the Idols*

"Most of the world's great souls have been lonely. Loneliness seems to be one price the saint must pay for his saintliness." – A.W. Tozer, *Best of Tozer*

"And he who sent me is with me. He has not left me alone, for I always do the things that are pleasing to him." – John 8:29

The Gospel story is filled with tales of lonely men, courageous leaders who, because they followed the call of God, were abandoned, maligned, misunderstood, even killed. Noah. Moses. David. The prophets. John the Baptist. Jesus. The Apostle Paul. All these men walked with God in an ungodly world, and paid a high relational price for it.

Loneliness can feel like severest pain. Over the ages, many prisoners have endured severe forms of physical torture, only to finally break when isolated through solitary confinement. If we are willing to be honest, many of us would admit that we would prefer to break our backs working for the kingdom of God rather than feel lonely for an extended period of time. Isolation is a particularly painful ache.

To be wild, we must be willing to be lonely. There's no other way to be masculine than to be courageously faithful to God. If Jesus has shown us anything, it's that being faithful to God in this world means you will walk alone at times. When Jesus did what His Father wanted, his family thought he was crazy, his friends deserted him, and his countrymen, the Israelites, wanted him killed. Jesus' faithfulness took him into painful, relational isolation. But, He was willing to go there. And we must be willing to go there, as well. In this day and age uncompromising faithfulness to God will lead us to high, cold, dangerous peaks. Alone. With the Lord.

DISCUSS TOGETHER

1) Why do faithful, courageous leaders often end up lonely?

2) Why do you think that loneliness is one of the hardest pains to endure?

3) Can you describe a time when you did the right thing, but ended up alone because of it?

4) Can you describe a time when you gave in and compromised doing the right thing in order not to feel lonely?

5) Faithful men can experience joy even when they are alone. What do you think the Wild Man enjoyed while living on the Wild Mountain?

6) Have someone read Romans 8:31-38. As Christians, the love and presence of God never leaves us. How can this truth keep us from feeling utterly alone in those moments when no person stands with us?

PRAY TOGETHER

Close in prayer asking God to give you the courage to be faithful, even if it means walking alone as a leader.

WILD MOUNTAIN TRIBE CHALLENGE

The challenge for this week is to spend one hour this week alone with God (praying, reading Scripture, and perhaps journaling). No cell phones. No television. No friends. No distractions. Just an hour alone with God.

– WEEK 11 –

"I'VE GOT YOUR BACK!"

READ OUT LOUD AS A GROUP:

"The only thing that makes battle psychologically tolerable is the brotherhood among soldiers. You need each other to get by." – Sebastian Junger

"And Elijah said to Elisha, 'Please stay here, for the LORD has sent me as far as Bethel.' But Elisha said, 'As the LORD lives, and as you yourself live, I will not leave you.' So they went down to Bethel." – 2 Kings 2:2

My son struck out three times during his first kid-pitch baseball game. I spent most of the game trying to think of what I would say to lift his spirits on the ride home. When we got into the truck, he exclaimed with excitement, "That was such a fun game, Dad!"

I was shocked. I almost drove the pickup into a light pole. I pulled over and turned around to look at him. "What made it a fun game, Buddy?"

He replied, "Didn't you see it? Carl got two hits! One went over the centerfielder's head!" Carl is Aidan's best friend, and because he did well, Aidan had a great night.

As men, we often struggle to make life-giving friendships because we feel driven to find our significance through our accomplishments. This achievement-oriented view of self makes us view our friends as measuring sticks, people to outperform in order to feel good about ourselves. This self-focus destroys our chance at true brotherhood. We can't love and support people that we feel we need to beat.

As we discussed last week, there will be times that we will walk alone. But not always. God has designed us for life-giving, soul-strengthening friendships, and the only way we can find these relationships is if we're living by faith in the grace of God. When we realize that we are fully significant and acceptable because of the finished work of Christ, we are able to quit looking to our performance and achievements to feel like we measure up. This faith, this grace of God, enables us to truly celebrate our friends' successes and mourn their losses.

DISCUSS TOGETHER

1) What are some ways that you have tried to best your friends in order to feel good about yourself? (I.e. through sports, work, academics, or possessions?)

2) Have someone read 1 Corinthians 13:1-7. How does the grace of God enable us to love others and enjoy solid, supportive friendships?

3) Have someone read Proverbs 17:17. Describe a time when a friend helped you go through a hard or stressful situation.

4) In *The Wild Man* fable, the Wild Man and the Ancient Man had a profound friendship. What role did their mission and work play their forming such

significant bonds?

5) What are some things you most appreciate about your friendships?

6) What are some things you'd like to see changed about your friendships?

PRAY TOGETHER

Have someone in your tribe read 1 Samuel 18:1-5. Pray together that God would give you an awareness of grace *so sincere* that it enables you to truly love and support your friends.

WILD MOUNTAIN TRIBE CHALLENGE

The challenge for this week is to write one friend a letter telling him what you most appreciate about him.

- WEEK 12 -

Choosing Heroes Carefully

READ OUT LOUD AS A GROUP:

"Our culture has filled our heads but emptied our hearts, stuffed our wallets but starved our wonder. It has fed our thirst for facts but not for meaning or mystery. It produces 'nice' people, not heroes." – Peter Kreeft, *Jesus-Shock*

"Brothers, join in imitating me, and keep your eyes on those who walk according to the example you have in us." – Philippians 3:17

"Do not be deceived: 'Bad company ruins good morals.'" – 1 Corinthians 15:33

The term "hero" comes from the ancient Greeks. A hero was someone who did something greater than what "normal humanity" was doing. Hercules performed twelve nearly impossible Labors. Achilles was the finest warrior of the Trojan War. Theseus was the Athenian hero who liberated his city from the tyranny of King Minos of Crete and his monstrous Minotaur. All three men were considered heroes because they stretched people's sense of possibility.

They did more than those around them and made others believe, "If my hero can be great, perhaps I can as well."

We need heroes today. We need examples of men who embody the qualities and virtues we would like to possess. As men aspiring to be wild and masculine, we need to find people who are representing various aspects of Christ—courage, justice, sacrifice, love, and honor—and we need to watch them, be inspired by them, and imitate them.

The question isn't whether or not we will choose heroes. The question is whether or not we will choose the right ones. If heroes give us vision and challenge us to imitate them, then we need to select the type of men we want to become. If we make a crass, vulgar man our hero, we will move toward crassness and vulgarity. Immanuel Kant said, "From the crooked timber of humanity, no straight thing was ever made."

As Wild Men, we need to choose Ancient Men as our heroes—men who are kind, hard-working, and honest. We should be drawn to men who are faithful to God and devoted to loving other people. If we follow and imitate masculine men, we will become masculine ourselves.

DISCUSS TOGETHER

1) Who are some of your heroes? Explain why.

2) Can you describe some of the ways that you have become like the men you most admire?

3) Have someone read Hebrews 11:13-16. Hebrews 11 is often referred to as the "Heroes of the Faith" chapter. According to these verses, what makes a

person a hero of the faith?

4) Apart from Jesus, our heroes will occasionally fail us. How can we use those moments of disillusionment to grow closer to God and deepen our faith?

5) Men *at any age* can be a hero to younger men. What are some ways in which the younger men in your tribe can be good and godly examples for the younger men in their lives?

PRAY TOGETHER

Pray for one another that you would choose the right heroes, and become the right kind of hero for other people.

WILD MOUNTAIN TRIBE CHALLENGE

The challenge for this week is to pick one of your heroes and pray for him each day that God would help him continue to be faithful and masculine.

- WEEK 13 -

WILD AND DISCIPLINED

READ OUT LOUD AS A GROUP:

"We must all suffer one of two things: the pain of discipline or the pain of regret, or disappointment."
— Jim Rohn

"No horse gets anywhere until he is harnessed. No steam or gas ever drives anything until it is confined. No Niagara is ever turned into light and power until it is tunneled. No life ever grows great until it is focused, dedicated, disciplined."
— Harry Emerson Fosdick

"Blessed is everyone who fears the LORD, who walks in his ways! You shall eat the fruit of the labor of your hands; you shall be blessed, and it shall be well with you."
— Psalm 128:1-2

It's time to live a wild, truly masculine life. The path forward for us is clear: we must fear the Lord, love His Word, and choose His ways over the ways of this world. To be wild, we must walk in the wisdom of God's designs, not fight against them. F.H. Farmer said, "If you go against the grain of the universe, you get splinters." [3]

Most of us went through Wild Mountain Tribe because we want to live free, strong, truly masculine lives. But, not everyone who goes through this journey will discover this truly wild and free existence. It's not because we don't understand these ideas; it's because we aren't willing to bend our knees and submit ourselves to the authority of God our Father. The great mystery that some of us will discover, but many will miss, is that true freedom exists in identifying ourselves as slaves to the Master of life, peace, strength, freedom, and truth. Only when we are bound to God will we be free to live on the Wild Mountain.

To bind ourselves to God is to obey Him no matter whether we fully understand, or enjoy, His commands. We must believe that He is Lord, and He is perfect in His plans for us. Perhaps it helps to consider the words of the great football coach, Tom Landry: "The job of a football coach is to make men do what they do not want to do in order to achieve what they always wanted to be." A wild man is wild because the world can't control him, yet he is fully submitted to the One who made him. This is the paradox of masculinity—the mystery that only the truly wild have discovered.

DISCUSS TOGETHER

1) Have someone read Romans 6:17-23. According to the Apostle Paul, is it possible not to be a slave to something? Can anyone actually be "their own man," in a way that they don't serve some master?

2) What does it look like for us to be "slaves of God" (Romans 6:22)?

3) Can you describe a man who lives a strong, humble life under the authority of God?

4) Describe an area of your life that you are trying to "go against the grain of the universe," by doing things your way instead of God's way.

5) What would it look like to submit to the Lord in that area, and choose to live according to His ways?

6) Elton Trueblood said, "Discipline is the price of freedom." For the older men in the tribe: How has this proven true over the course of your lifetime?

PRAY TOGETHER

Pray together that God would give you a vision for what it looks like to submit to His authority and choose to obey His commands.

WILD MOUNTAIN TRIBE CHALLENGE

The challenge for this week is to start each day this week on your knees, praying that God would give you a heart to submit to Him.

---

3) H.H. Farmer, as quoted in Eugene Peterson, *A Long Obedience in the Same Direction: Discipleship in an Instant Society* (Downers Grove: InterVarsity Press, 2000), 121.

– WEEK 14 –

TORCH-BEARING

READ OUT LOUD AS A GROUP:

"Women can change the embryo to a boy, but only men can change the boy into a man. Initiators say that boys need a second birth, this time a birth from men."
— Robert Bly, *Iron John*

"I believe that what we become depends on what our fathers teach us at odd moments, when they aren't trying to teach us. We are formed by little scraps of wisdom."
— Umberto Eco

"...and what you have heard from me in the presence of many witnesses entrust to faithful men who will be able to teach others also." — 2 Timothy 2:2

Remember the days when men were men? They dressed with self-respect and style. They honored their elders. They opened doors for women and greeted each other with a strong handshake. They worked hard and took pride in their careers. And they weren't afraid to move out of their parent's house, get married, remain faithful to their wife, have children, and teach their children how to grow up big and strong. Remember those days? You might not... they were quite some time ago. Today, more and more boys are refusing to travel the ancient paths of masculinity, and in large part because more and more men are failing to show them the way.

In *The Wild Man* fable, the Wild Man receives his final mark only after he passes the torch to Keon. A wild man doesn't merely enjoy his own masculinity; he also empowers younger men to enjoy theirs as well. All truly wild men take their responsibility to instruct, correct, rebuke, and train others as seriously as they take their own call to be wild.

We—who desire to be courageously wild, ferociously loving, entirely sacrificial, and bravely faithful—must teach the young men in our lives how to join us. We must be wild, and give them a vision for true masculinity. Stephen Mansfield writes, "All it takes for a contagious manly culture to form is for one genuine man to live out a genuine manhood."[4] We must be the torchbearers a new generation of wild men need us to be.

DISCUSS TOGETHER

1) Describe one or two men who have been torchbearers for you, helping cast a vision for wild masculinity.

2) Describe a few opportunities that you currently have to be a torchbearer to other men.

3) Many older men do not feel adequate to be torchbearers for younger men. What are some reasons why older men disengage from this responsibility?

4) Older men can only teach and cast a vision for masculinity if they are willing to spend time with younger men. What are some obstacles that seem to prevent older men and younger men spending time together?

5) Have someone read Deuteronomy 6:4-9. What role does God's Word play in how we older men pass along masculinity to younger men?

PRAY TOGETHER

Pray for the desire and the opportunity to be faithful torchbearers.

WILD MOUNTAIN TRIBE CHALLENGE

The challenge for this week is to write a letter to a younger man in your life describing a few of the lessons God has taught you over the past fourteen weeks about being a faithful, wild man.

---

4) Stephen Mansfield, *Mansfield's Book of Manly Men: An Utterly Invigorating Guide to Being Your Most Masculine Self* (Nashville: Nelson Books, 2013), 34.

Wild Mountain Feast

Unlike other adventures, our journey to the Wild Mountain never ends. We like checklists. We like to make a box, mark it, and declare, "I'm done. Time to move on to the next box." We must resist the urge to think this way about our journey toward masculinity. The second we stop growing and changing is the moment we cease to be wild. A truly masculine man seeks to be more faithful and masculine tomorrow than he is today.

That being said, we have traveled far together through difficult terrain. We have ascended the Wild Mountain and it's time to celebrate. It's time to slow down and enjoy the view together. Most importantly, it's time for us older men to initiate the young men in our tribe into the fraternity of wild men. It's time to feast together.

There is great freedom within each tribe to personalize this Wild Mountain Feast. Depending on your interests, you may make or buy personal gifts, add various rituals, and plan a meal that you most enjoy. For some, the Wild Mountain Feast might consist entirely of meat. For others, it might involve seven courses. This is your Wild Mountain Feast, so enjoy planning it the way your tribe prefers.

For your consideration, here are a few suggestions for your Wild Mountain Feast:

Have the Older Serve the Younger.

The older men should plan the evening, choose the location and menu, and serve the younger men. You might hold the feast in a restaurant, at your tribe's special meeting spot, at a state park, or in a backyard.

Give a Gift.

The initiation from boyhood into manhood is a life-changing event, one that the young men will remember the rest of their lives. Consider giving each young man a gift that will last the rest of their lives. This could be a homemade knife if you're a metal worker, a cutting board if you're a chef, a shotgun if you're a hunter, or a hammer if you're a carpenter. The goal isn't to give an expensive gift; it's to pass along something personal and meaningful.

Acknowledge a Quality.

Have each older man in your tribe write a short letter to each younger man acknowledging one trait that they most respect about him. Give these letters as a gift during the celebration.

Pronounce a Blessing.

Have each older man read a passage of Scripture and pray a blessing upon the young man he journeyed with to the Wild Mountain. Alternatively, this Scripture and blessing could be written down and given to the young man during the celebration.

ACKNOWLEDGMENTS

I am immeasurably thankful to my two beautiful, bright-eyed daughters, Kate and Claire. These young women own just as much of my heart as does their brother Aidan. Yet, to complete this project I had to spend a disproportionate amount of time thinking specifically about how to parent Aidan. Kate and Claire never complained about this imbalance; rather, they consistently displayed excitement and support for this project. I'm also amazed at their ability to keep a secret—they knew about *The Wild Man* and *Wild Mountain Tribe* for two years and managed to keep Aidan in the dark until I gave him these books as a gift.

This book for men would be missing many of its insights had it not been for the wise contributions of my wife, Jamie, and my mother, Mary Pipher. The fact that I was given the gift of being related to not one, but two, brilliant thinkers and readers proves that the universe does not spread its blessings out equally. My favorite time of the day is when Jamie and I make dinner together and sort through the things of life. Many of the ideas in *The Wild Man* and *Wild Mountain Tribe* were fleshed out with her over a cutting board, the smell of garlic, two glasses of Pinot Noir, and Van Morrison singing in the background. She is my true companion, and to quote Van, "the heavens open every time she smiles."

I want to specifically acknowledge my mother for her support and contribution. While my mom and I, in many ways, share the same soul, we hold vastly different world-views. I am a Christian and a conservative, and I primarily write about men's issues. She is a Buddhist and a liberal, and has been a strong voice within the feminist movement. Yet, mom has read, edited, and zealously supported each one of my writing projects, including this one. In this polarized, angry day when dehumanizing the other side is so terribly common, her example is worth celebrating. I have known few people who share my mom's desire and her ability to transcend significant differences in order to find common ground and ways to support one another. I am honored to be her son.

There are two men, in particular, who have put flesh on the abstract idea of masculinity for me: my friend and mentor, Bryan Clark, and my father-in-law, RB Drickey. Both men happen to be bald; yet, when it comes to being strong, faithful, and wild, they are two of the hairiest men I know. I could have illustrated each chapter of *Wild Mountain Tribe* with stories from their lives.

I'm also thankful for my dad, Jim Pipher. He taught me how to pitch a baseball, tell a joke, and oppose a racist or sexist comment. Also, it is no small task for a rational ISTJ to patiently bear with a relational ENFP, and he has been at this work for over forty years.

I am deeply indebted to Heartland's elders, pastors, and staff. These friends gave me the time and permission to write *The Wild Man* and *Wild Mountain Tribe*. I also want to mention the role that one of my best friends, Jeff Brehm, played in this writing process. Long before *The Wild Man* became a file on my computer, during a road trip to our favorite trout stream, Jeff asked me to tell him a story. I told him about *The Wild Man*. When I finished, Jeff wiped a tear from his cheek. His enthusiastic response to that first telling of this fable is what motivated me to start writing.

I'm also grateful for my readers: Kate Pipher, Claire Pipher, JJ Springer, Bryan Clark, Matt Mitchell, and Linda Peterson, my type-setter and one of my all-time favorite vocalists: Reynold Peterson, and my illustrator: Angie Johnson. These skilled friends turned lead into gold, and it was an honor to work alongside them.

These writing projects were undoubtedly influenced by the books I read and the music I listened to these past three years. I particularly enjoyed reading *Iron John* by Robert Bly, *Playing God* by Andy Crouch, *The Boys in the Boat* by Daniel James

Brown, *Genesis* by Bruce Waltke, *Tribe* by Sebastian Junger, *Last Child in the Woods* by Richard Louv, and *Boone* by Robert Morgan. Music-wise, I continually enjoyed *Home* by Josh Garrels, *Ten Thousand Days* by Bebo Norman, *The Next Thing* by Geoff Moore, *As Sure as the Sun* by Ellie Holcomb, *Into the Wild* (soundtrack) by Eddie Vedder, and every album by Josh Ritter, Mumford & Sons, The Avett Brothers, Gregory Alan Isakov, The Lumineers, Bon Iver, Van Morrison, and Andrew Peterson.

To purchase either *Wild Mountain Tribe* or *The Wild Man* fable, visit:

www.thewildmountain.com
www.zekepipher.com